GIVE IT SOME

THOUGHT

Also by the authors:

The Conversation Piece
The Christmas Conversation Piece
The Conversation Piece 2
Think Twice!
Toe Tappin' Trivia
Have You Ever . . .
The Talk of the Tee
The Check Book
Who We Are
The Christmas Letters

GIVE IT SOME
THOUGHT

?

Quotes to Remember & Questions to Ponder

Bret Nicholaus and Paul Lowrie

The Question Guys™
Bestselling authors of *The Conversation Piece*

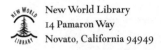 New World Library
14 Pamaron Way
Novato, California 94949

Cover design: Mary Ann Casler
Text design and layout: Mary Ann Casler

Library of Congress Cataloging-in-Publication Data
Nicholaus, Bret.
 Give it some thought : quotes to remember & questions to ponder / Bret Nicholaus and Paul Lowrie.
  p. cm.
 Includes index.
 ISBN 1-57731-159-0 (alk. paper)
 I. Conduct of life—Quotations, maxims, etc. I. Lowrie, Paul. II. Title.
BF637.C5 N53 2001
158.1—dc21   00-013262

First printing, April 2001
ISBN 1-57731-159-0
Printed in Canada on acid-free, recycled paper
Distributed to the trade by Publishers Group West

10 9 8 7 6 5 4 3 2 1

The answers you get
depend upon the questions you ask.

— Thomas Kuhn

Welcome

Look around any office, on any refrigerator door, in any wallet, at the start of any book. Chances are pretty good that you will find a short, inspirational quotation — a sentence or two to remind us of what's important. Powerful, inspirational quotes serve as rally points for all our divergent thoughts, giving us focus when we need it most. Futhermore, great quotations can motivate or change us like virtually nothing else.

Yet how many times do we post a quote on our bulletin board, read it again and again, but never really *act* on it? Much like a sermon or motivational speech (many of which revolve around inspiring quotations), a great quote does little good if we don't put its words into practice. Often this requires an outside challenge. As the authors of several popular question books, we began to wonder what would happen if we combined a well-rounded sampling of extraordinary quotations with truly thought-provoking, action-oriented *questions*. It seemed to us that the two themes — quotations and questions — were beautifully complementary; when properly mixed, they could inspire deep introspection, which could then spur life-changing action.

Thus, *Give It Some Thought* was born. Each page of this unique book provides a quote worth remembering, immediately followed by a series of questions to help you apply that quotation to your own life. You can easily enjoy *Give It Some Thought* for the memorable quotes alone, or you can leaf through the pages solely to answer the stimulating questions. The most fulfilling way to experience this book, however, is to carefully consider each quotation and then give the corresponding questions some serious and heartfelt thought.

Each quote and its questions lay the foundation for entertaining discussions with your friends and family members; it's always fun to learn how *they* would answer the questions. But we created this book ultimately to help you discover more about yourself and the life *you* are living: What are the greatest life lessons you've learned so far? Where is your life headed? What must change for you to live the life you've imagined? What are your inspirations — and your aspirations? Who are the people who have had the biggest impact on the person you've become, and who are the people *you* have changed? As you weave your way through the pages of *Give It Some Thought,* hundreds of questions like these will move you to reach deep into your soul and seek the truth about who you really are — and all that you still wish to become.

Enjoy,

Bret Nicholaus and Paul Lowrie

GIVE IT SOME
THOUGHT

I make myself rich by making my wants few.

— Henry David Thoreau

In what ways do people actually become "rich"
by making their wants few?

Have you ever given something up and found, as a result,
that you felt liberated or freer than before?

How do you personally differentiate between wants and needs?
Do you consider some things as needs that others would consider wants?

Be honest: On a scale of one to ten, where one is unimportant
and ten very important, how important is it that you acquire
more and more things as you continue through life?

In what ways do you feel "richer" than other people you know?

How much easier and simpler would your life be if you were willing
to part with some of your current "wants"?

A long life may not be good enough,
but a good life is long enough.

— Benjamin Franklin

Would you rather die at fifty, having lived an extremely satisfying and successful life, or live to be one hundred, having experienced little happiness and few real highlights in life?

What three components above all others are necessary for creating the "good life"?

If you were to die today, what would be your life's greatest satisfaction?

If you were to die today, could you die at peace with yourself and the life you've lived?

*Most people spend more time and energy
going around problems than
trying to solve them.*

— Henry Ford

In general, do you avoid problems or obstacles in your life or do you confront them as soon as possible?

Can you think of any recent issue or problem you've been trying to circumvent rather than solve?

What in particular is keeping you from dealing with this problem?

How much better would your life be if you tackled this issue head-on?

*To be blind is bad, but worse it is
to have eyes and not to see.*

— Helen Keller

What is something intangible that you tend to notice
but others typically fail to see or appreciate?
Why do you think you have a heightened awareness of it?

Can you identify something *tangible* you tend to notice
(or look for) that most others fail to see?

In your opinion, what issue or problem in today's society
are many people blind to?
Have you taken any steps to make others aware of this issue?

If you knew that beginning tomorrow you would be blind for the rest
of your life, what — not whom — would you want to see
more than anything else in the whole world?

One person with passion is better than forty who are merely interested.

— Tom Connellan, from *Inside the Magic Kingdom*

In what ways could one passionate person actually be more beneficial than forty interested ones?

Can you think of at least three things in life you truly have a passion for?
Can other people sense this passion?
Does your passion for these things make you better at them?

In what ways does passion differ from persistence, or are they the same?
If they are different, which is more valuable?

Do you believe that passion for one's job is indispensable?
Why or why not?

Can you think of companies where employees tend to be passionate about their jobs? Are these companies successful?

*Remove failure as an option
and your chances for success
become infinitely better.*

— Joan Lunden

Do you tend to approach situations expecting obstacles or opportunities?

Do you know people who approach situations assuming they won't
excel or that they'll fail? What outcomes have they experienced?

Why would simply eliminating failure as an option increase
your chances for ultimate success?

Like so many things in life, it's often easier said than done. So how does a
person practically and effectively *remove* failure as a potential outcome?

For you, what does it mean to fail? Given your definition,
have you ever truly failed at something?

*If all our misfortunes were laid in
one common heap whence everyone must take
an equal portion, most people would be
contented to take their own and depart.*

— Socrates

What are some problems your friends have had that you can't
even imagine having?

Do you think some of your friends would gladly trade
their own misfortunes for yours?
How quick would you be to trade your problems for theirs?

If you asked your friends, would they guess that your life is easier
or more difficult than it actually is?

Why do we tend to see the grass as greener on the other side of the fence?

How exciting are your dreams?
Most people don't aim too high and miss —
they aim too low and hit!

— Bob Moawad

What dreams have you already fulfilled?
What are some dreams that you're still shooting for?

Have you set your dreams high or low?

Do you prefer to set dreams for yourself that are easy to achieve,
or dreams that are only realized through time and hard work?

What are the advantages and disadvantages
of aiming low with your dreams?
What about aiming high?

Most folks are about as happy as they make up their minds to be.

— Abraham Lincoln

On a scale of one to ten, how happy a person would you say you are?

What things in life make you happiest?
Do you pursue these things diligently?

How well do you manage negative thoughts? What do you generally do when discouraging or negative thoughts enter your mind?

Who is the happiest person you know?
Do you have any idea what their secret to happiness is?

If people who have virtually nothing can be happy,
why do so many of us who have everything we need
find it so difficult to be happy?

Nearly all men can stand adversity,
but if you want to test a man's character,
give him power.

— Abraham Lincoln

What would be a greater test of *your* character:
facing extreme adversity or being given a tremendous amount of power?

Do you believe that some degree of corruption is
an unavoidable by-product of power?

What are some specific ways in which having power
would test the average person's character?

If you were suddenly given a lot of power (becoming the boss of an entire
company, for example), how would it change you?
How might people actually benefit from your being in control?
What risks would they face?

Better keep yourself clean and bright;
you are the window through which
you must see the world.

— George Bernard Shaw

What is *your* general view of the world?
Have you always had this view?

How clean is your "window"? What do you suppose is meant by
"keep yourself clean and bright"?

How does a person's particular lifestyle affect their view of the world?

Endeavor to live so that when you die,
even the undertaker will be sorry.

— Mark Twain

What is one thing you just know people will say about you after you're gone?

For what reasons — big or small — would people miss you if you died?

What are some of the qualities shared by people
who are greatly missed after they're gone?

In your opinion, what would be the noblest reason
for a person to be missed after they die?

Aside from family members who have died,
who is someone you truly miss? Why?

What would you like to change about yourself in order
to leave a better legacy behind?

Watch your thoughts; they become words.
Watch your words; they become actions.
Watch your actions; they become habits.
Watch your habits; they become character.
Watch your character; it becomes your destiny.

— Frank Outlaw

Of these five phrases, which one has the greatest potential
to get you into trouble?

Which phrase do you believe is the most difficult for people
across the board?

Can you trace a specific thought you once had all the way through Frank
Outlaw's list, proving that it really can lead to your destiny?

How does one's character open the door to destiny?

Lots of people want to ride with you in the limo, but what you want is someone who will take the bus with you when the limo breaks down.

— Oprah Winfrey

Have you surrounded yourself with friends who will be there for you if and when the going gets tough?

What's the best measure of a true friend?
What qualities do you look for in people?

If you could keep only one of your friends — *only one* — whom would you choose and why?

I have had more trouble with myself than with any other person I have ever met.

— Dwight L. Moody

If you had to list your three biggest flaws, what would they be?
What are you doing to correct these shortcomings?

What traits do you tend to judge in others?
In what areas of life are you especially hard on *yourself*?

Generally speaking, do you consider yourself a better person
than most people you know?
Why or why not?

If a small thing has the power to make you angry,
does that not indicate something about your size?

— Sydney J. Harris

What are some seemingly small or insignificant things that tend to upset
you? What about these things bothers you so much?

What is the smallest thing you can remember
making you really, really angry?

Do you tend to cope better with larger issues or with smaller ones?

How do you react to larger, more difficult problems in life?

On a scale of one to ten (where one is very poor and ten is very good),
how would you rate your anger management?

I don't know what your destiny will be,
but one thing I know: the only ones among you
who will be truly happy are those who will
have sought and found how to serve.

— Albert Schweitzer

Can you think of a specific time when helping someone
made you feel really good inside?

In what ways do you find joy in serving others?

What type of service do you find the most rewarding?

Do you prefer to serve others through giving money, time, or talent?
Why?

Be totally honest with yourself:
Do you personally find more happiness in giving or receiving?

*Statistically, 100 percent of
the shots you don't take don't go in.*

— Wayne Gretzsky

*You can't steal second base
and keep one foot on first.*

— Frederick B. Wilson

Are you afraid of failure? Why or why not?

Are you willing to fail at something
just to say that you gave it your best shot?

In hindsight, what was one "shot" you wish you had taken
but regrettably didn't?

What is one thing you've always wanted to do
or accomplish but haven't yet?
What specifically is holding you back?
What must you do to overcome this obstacle?

Nothing in the world can take
the place of persistence.
Talent will not; nothing is more common
than unsuccessful people with talent.
Genius will not; unrewarded genius is
almost a proverb. Education will not;
the world is full of educated failures.
Persistence and determination
alone are omnipotent.

— Calvin Coolidge

Do you possess more talent, genius, education, or persistence?

Why is persistence such a powerful weapon?

Can a person become a success without persistence?

Who are some of the more persistent and determined people you know?
Do you consider them successful?

When you reach for the stars,
you may not quite get one,
but you won't come up with
a handful of mud either.

— Leo Burnett

How willingly do you accept results that differ from your expectations?

Can you think of a specific time when you strived to achieve one thing but ended up with something radically different?

Can you think of another time when you fell short of your goal but the process yielded positive results anyway?

Does setting very high expectations potentially lead to too much disappointment?

It is better to be boldly decisive
and risk being wrong
than to agonize at length
and be right too late.

— Marilyn Moats Kennedy

Do you tend to act on things spontaneously or do you carefully think things through? What are the benefits and risks of each approach?

Can you recall a time when you delayed taking action just a little too long, only to miss out on a great opportunity?

Can you recall a time when you were absolutely sure that you were right and ended up being wrong? How did you feel?

Do you think that most people act too quickly or too slowly when it comes to decision-making? Why do you think most people act this way?

God gives every bird his worm,
but He does not throw it into the nest.

— Swedish proverb

Do you tend to wait for opportunities to come to you,
or do you go out and find them?

What are the advantages of having to work hard for something,
of not being handed things on a silver platter?

What is one thing you just know is out there waiting for you
if you would only go out and pursue it?

*Some men storm imaginary Alps
all their lives and die in the foothills
cursing difficulties which do not exist.*

— Edgar Watson Howe

As the saying goes, do you tend to "make mountains out of molehills"?

Are you more likely to downplay a problem or exaggerate it
when talking to other people?

Be honest with yourself: Which of your current difficulties are probably
not nearly as bad as you make them out to be?

Which of your difficulties have been products of your own doing?

I cried because I had no shoes
until I met a man who had no feet.

— Persian saying

What do you tend to complain about unjustifiably?

In what ways do you think others have it better than you?
In what ways do you have it better than they?

What circumstances, when you see them,
make you realize just how good you really have it?

If you had to name just one encounter or experience you've had
that put your life in proper perspective — making you realize how
fortunate you are — which one would you pick?

In this world there are only two tragedies.
One is not getting what one wants,
and the other is getting it.

— Oscar Wilde

What is one thing you've always wanted but still don't have?

In what ways, or under what circumstances, could getting what one wants be deemed a "tragedy"?

Have you ever been devastated because you didn't get something or because something didn't work out as you had planned? Have you ever gotten something in life (tangible or intangible) you thought you really wanted, only to discover that your life was better without it?

Can you think of any instances, either in history or with people you've known, where someone got what they wanted, with tragic results?

*Always bear in mind that
your own resolution to succeed
is more important than any other factor.*

— Abraham Lincoln

**Whether you think you can or think you can't,
you're right.**

— Henry Ford

To what extent do you believe in mind over matter?

Do you generally tend to think more along the lines of
"I can" or "I can't"?

To which current challenges or opportunities are you saying "I can"?
To what are you currently saying "I can't"?

To which past challenges or opportunities did you resolve in the very
beginning that you would succeed no matter what?
Were you indeed successful?

Who are some famous people in sports, business, politics, or entertainment who always seem to maintain an "I can" attitude?
Can you learn anything specific from these people?

Keep away from people who try to belittle your ambitions. Small people always do that, but the really great make you feel that you, too, can become great.

— Mark Twain

Have you ever met someone who made you feel insignificant
or foolish about your dreams or goals?
How did you react after hearing what they had to say?

How important is it for you personally to be encouraged by others
when making decisions or taking action?

Have you ever known someone who really encouraged you
when you were down?

Who are some people who have made you feel important
throughout your life?

Who have *you* encouraged to pursue their dreams?

Do you believe in encouraging people even if their ideas seem bound to
fail? Where and how do you draw the line between being honest and
being encouraging?

A certain amount of opposition
is a great help to a person.
Kites rise against, not with the wind.

— John Neal

In what ways is opposition — to a cause, goal,
or dream — a good thing?

At what point do you think opposition
becomes a hindrance rather than a help?

Think of your greatest successes or achievements. What was the greatest
opposition to success in each case? Would you have been as successful if
those obstacles hadn't existed?

Success is how high you bounce
when you hit bottom.

— General George S. Patton

Do you think a person needs to first overcome serious adversity
or tragedy to be truly successful?

Have you ever bounced back from something truly difficult?
How did you do it?

Do you think that character is better tested through failure or success?
Why?

Success isn't a result of spontaneous combustion.
You must learn to set yourself on fire.

— Arnold H. Glasow

Do you consider yourself a self-motivated person?

Athletes often pump themselves up before big games.
How do you motivate yourself when you need to?

What are some steps you've taken recently
to improve your chances for future success?
What is the single most important step you've taken thus far?

*Establishing goals is all right
if you don't let them deprive you
of interesting detours.*

— Doug Larson

Do you believe in establishing goals for yourself?

Do you prefer to set short-term goals or long-term goals?

How disappointed do you become if you don't meet your goals?

How is goal-setting potentially bad? In what ways is it good?

Have you personally taken any interesting detours on the way to your goals? Where did these detours lead you?

The key to everything is patience.
You get the chicken by hatching the egg,
not by smashing it.

— Arnold H. Glasow

Do you generally consider yourself a patient or impatient person?
Are you patient in some areas of life and impatient in others?
In what specific areas of life would it behoove you to have more patience?

Can you think of a time when your willingness to be patient with
something or someone produced wonderful results?

Have you ever completely lost your patience with something or someone?
What was the result?

Why do you think that patience is such an important virtue to learn?
Do you agree or disagree with Glasow that the key to everything
is, indeed, patience?

The art of being happy lies in the power of extracting happiness from common things.

— Henry Ward Beecher

What simple things in life have made you truly happy?
What are some simple pleasures you can't imagine living without?

Do you try to appreciate life's smallest moments,
extracting as much pleasure from them as possible?

What is the simplest thing in your life that provides you with
an immense amount of satisfaction, peace, or joy?

If you were to make a list of the ten things in life that make you
happiest, how many of them would be material?
How many things on your list would be considered ordinary
or mundane by other peoples' standards?

Perhaps it would be a good idea,
fantastic as it sounds,
to muffle every telephone,
stop every motor and halt
all activity for one hour some day
just to give people a chance
to ponder for a few minutes
on what it is all about, why they are living
and what they really want.

— James Truslow Adams

What do you think are the biggest distractions in peoples' lives?

What is the biggest distraction in your own life right now?

In what ways does the business and "busyness" of today's lifestyle con-
tribute to a less satisfying life overall? In what specific ways did those
who came before us have it better?

Do you ever take the time to sit in total silence and reflect on your life?
If so, what was revealed to you in these quiet, contemplative moments?

First I was dying to finish high school
and start college.
And then I was dying to finish college
and start working.
And then I was dying to marry
and have children.
And then I was dying for my children to grow
old enough so I could get back to work.
And then I was dying to retire.
And now I am dying...
and suddenly realize that I forgot to live.

— Author unknown

Do you generally live your life for the present or for the future?

In what ways do you think it's important to live in the here and now?
In what ways is it important to look ahead?

Have you ever missed out on something because you were too focused
on the future rather than the present?
In hindsight, what are some things you wish you had embraced
more fully while you were experiencing them?

What are some things throughout your life you just couldn't wait to do?
Were they everything you expected them to be?

If you died today, what would be your biggest regret?

*It is one of the most beautiful
compensations of this life
that no man can sincerely try to help another
without helping himself.*

— Ralph Waldo Emerson

*Help others get ahead.
You will always stand taller
with someone else on your shoulders.*

— Bob Moawad

In helping others, how does a person help himself in the process?

Do you feel better — or "bigger" — after you help someone?

Whose life or career have you helped?

Whom could you help get ahead right now?
What could you do to help them out?

What was the most rewarding thing you ever did for someone else?

What is something you would love to do for someone at some point but haven't yet?

*Compare what you want
with what you have,
and you'll be unhappy;
compare what you have
with what you deserve,
and you'll be happy.*

—— Evan Esar

What three things do you really want in your life but don't have?

To what extent would you feel unfulfilled if you never got them?

When you stop and think about what you have in life,
are you basically content or desirous for more?

Do you think that you deserve most of the things that you already have?
Why or why not?

Do you know people who, in your opinion, deserve more in life than
what they now have?

Do you know people who, in your opinion, do *not* deserve all they now have?

A life is not important except in the impact it has on other lives.

— Jackie Robinson

Do you think people can consider their lives successful even if they haven't helped others along the way? Why or why not?

Do you ever stop to think about the impact you currently have or have had on peoples' lives? In what ways have you influenced other people?

Who has had the greatest impact on your life?
Have you ever told this person?

If you could change the world in some way,
what would you want to do most of all?

Many a man has found the acquisition of wealth only a change, not an end, of miseries.

— Lucius Annaeus Seneca

Why do you think so many people believe that money will solve their problems? How are they likely wrong?

What are three problems you believe wealth can lead to, either directly or indirectly?

What problems have you witnessed among people who have a lot of money?

If you suddenly came into a lot of money, what would be your biggest *worry* about how it might affect you or your life?

One cannot collect all the beautiful shells on the beach. One can collect only a few, and they are more beautiful if they are few.

— Anne Morrow Lindbergh

What does this metaphor say to us about life?

In what ways is it better to have fewer rather than many "shells"? Do you believe in the "less is more" theory?

Metaphorically, what are some of your life's most beautiful shells?

The secret of genius is to carry
the spirit of the child into old age.

— Aldous Huxley

In what ways, if any, do you think you exhibit a childlike spirit?

For what reasons would a childlike spirit be such a wise thing
to embrace as you get older?

What are some things that adults would do well to learn from children?

What is the most important lesson you have ever learned from a child?

*The acceptance of boundaries and limits
is the gateway to freedom.*

— Phil Jackson, from *Sacred Hoops*

*Do not let what you **cannot** do
interfere with what you **can** do.*

— John Wooden

Do you recognize your own limitations? How willing are you to admit that you just cannot do some things? What are some of those things?

Has your inability to do one thing ever kept you from doing something you *did* have the ability to do?

In what ways is it important to know your limitations in your life or career?

How can recognizing your inabilities actually help to improve the skills you already have?

Vitality shows not only in the ability to persist but also in the ability to start over.

— F. Scott Fitzgerald

Why do you think that starting over is so hard?

How willing are you to admit to yourself that you've failed at something? How quick are you to get going again after you've failed?

How do you know when you should still be holding on to something or when it's time to let it go and try something new?

The best thing about the future
is that it comes only one day at a time.

— Abraham Lincoln

What are the advantages and disadvantages of looking at life
with Lincoln's philosophy?

Can you think of situations where "one day at a time" is actually
a very difficult way to think?
When would this outlook be helpful and reassuring?

Do you tend to focus more on final destinations — the future — or on
the journeys themselves — the day-by-day happenings?

Progress is our ability to complicate simplicity.

— Thor Heyerdahl

If our quality of life is supposedly the best it's ever been, why do you
think we have less and less time to actually enjoy it?

What are a few ways in which we were better off 150 years ago?
What about 50 years ago?

In what ways has progress actually set us back?

What particular product or invention more than any other
has complicated your own life?

What is something that most people consider a convenience
that you regard as a pain-in-the-neck?

Considering all the ramifications, if you could un-invent any one thing in
the world for the purpose of simplifying life, what would it be?

*I love best to have each thing in its season,
doing without it at all other times.*

— Henry David Thoreau

How is it good to do without things for periods of time?

What are some things in your life that are more enjoyable
because you experience them so rarely?

Is there anything that you experience during a certain time of the year
that you wish you could have all year long? If you did have it all the time,
would your enjoyment of it possibly diminish?

What is more enjoyable for you personally: the anticipation of something
— like a season or a holiday — or the actual thing itself?

To consider Thoreau's quote literally, what does each of the four seasons
offer that makes it uniquely special to you?

Thinking is the hardest work there is —
which is probably the reason so few engage in it.

— Henry Ford

Do you believe that you spend more or less time thinking than the average person?

Why do you believe people are often so reluctant to stop and really think about something?

What particular issues or subjects do you expend the most energy thinking about?

Are there any issues or topics that you basically refuse to think about? Why?

When you need to do some serious thinking, what environment works best for you?

What is the most difficult thing you've ever had to think about? Did thinking about it drain your energy?

If you could get everyone in the world to think very carefully about one subject for one hour, what subject would you choose?

*The opportunities of man are limited
only by his imagination,
but so few have imagination that there
are ten thousand fiddlers to one composer.*

— Charles F. Kettering

*Imagination is more important
than knowledge.*

— Albert Einstein

Who are three people in history whose imagination you envy?

Be honest: On a scale of one to ten, where one is very unimaginative and ten extremely imaginative, how imaginative do you think you are?

What is the most creative idea you've ever had?
Did you follow through on it?

Would you rather hire someone who is extremely knowledgeable or extremely imaginative?

What are the differences between someone who has great intelligence and someone who has great imagination?
Which do you believe will get someone further in life?

If you could create or invent anything you wanted — anything at all — what would it be?

The happiness of your life depends upon the quality of your thoughts.

— Marcus Antonius

In what ways is your own degree of happiness directly related to your day-to-day thoughts?

What do you tend to think about most often? Why?

Generally, do the things you think about cheer you up or bring you down?

What is one daily thought you could focus on that would increase your happiness?

*Without heroes, we are all plain people
and don't know how far we can go.*

— Bernard Malamud, from *The Natural*

Growing up, who was your biggest hero?
Who is your biggest hero today?

For you, personally, do heroes truly motivate and challenge you
to reach a higher level? Why or why not?

What characteristics or traits do you look for in a real-life hero?

In your opinion, who is the greatest real-life hero of all time?
What can we learn from this person?

The less you talk,
the more you're listened to.

— Abigail Van Buren

When is silence truly golden? In the long run, what are the distinct advantages of speaking only when it is absolutely necessary?

Do you tend to say too much or too little? What about most other people?

Can you think of any specific times when keeping quiet would have gotten you a lot farther than speaking out did?

Are there certain topics which, when raised, you feel the need to speak up about? Why or why not? Do you think one gains or loses respect by speaking out early and often?

*The most important thing in communication
is to hear what isn't being said.*

— Peter Drucker

How good are you at "reading between the lines" when people
are communicating with you?

How well tuned are you with people's nonverbal cues?
How do these cues sometimes say more than the spoken word?

Do you ask others to clarify and qualify
when they say something you don't fully understand?

Do you try to say exactly what you mean or
do you leave much open to interpretation?

In what specific ways could the clarity of your communication
be improved?

*Sainthood emerges when you can listen
to someone else's tale of woe and not respond
with a description of your own.*

— Andrew V. Mason, MD

Do you notice when other people try to "better" your stories?
Are you aware of it when you do the same thing?

Why do you think so many people find it necessary to "one-up" others'
stories? Do you personally find it hard to just listen
without responding with a story of your own?

Why do you think Dr. Mason considers the ability to withhold
your own story such a great virtue?

*Sandwich every bit of criticism
between two layers of praise.*

— Mary Kay Ash, from *Mary Kay on People Management*

Why is it so important to dole out plenty of praise?

In what ways is praising somebody else also helpful to the person
doing the praising?

Do you tend to heed Mary Kay's advice?

Are you better at serving up criticism or praise? Why?

How do you personally respond — internally and externally — when
you receive criticism? What about when you receive praise?

When criticism is necessary, do you think there is an appropriate way
to deliver it? How?

Speak when you are angry and you will make the best speech you will ever regret.

— Ambrose Bierce

How good are you at restraining your tongue in moments of anger?

Have you ever said something in anger that you truly regretted later?

What are the short- and long-term advantages of waiting to speak until things have calmed down?

What could you do to prevent saying hurtful or foolish things in moments of anger?

In rivers, the water that you touch
is the last of what has passed
and the first of that which comes:
so it is with present time.

— Leonardo da Vinci

What does this quote have to say about yesterday? And tomorrow?

What do the past and the future share?

What is the unique beauty of this very day?

Why does water serve as such a perfect metaphor for time?

*Courage is not the towering oak
that sees storms come and go;
it is the fragile blossom
that opens in the snow.*

— Alice Mackenzie Swaim

What does this quote say about courage?
Is the author's view of courage typical or rare?

Who are the courageous people you have known in your life?
Were they more like the oak or the tender blossom?

Which of these two types of courage would you rather manifest?
Which type, in truth, do you actually exhibit?

What would be a practical example of oak-like courage?
. . . and blossom-like courage?

The pessimist complains about the wind;
the optimist expects it to change;
the realist adjusts the sails.

—William Arthur Ward

Be honest with yourself: Are you a pessimist, an optimist, or a realist?

How do you think other people who know you would categorize you?

In what areas of life do you tend to be more
of a pessimist, optimist, and realist?
In each situation, why do you lean one way or another?

What do you think is the greatest danger in being a pessimist?
. . . an optimist? . . . a realist?

When some external event raises your spirits and you think good days are preparing for you, do not believe it. It can never be so. Nothing can bring you peace but yourself.

— Ralph Waldo Emerson

What are some external events in your life
that have really made you happy?

What are some possessions in your life that have brought you
a lot of satisfaction? How long-lasting was that satisfaction?

On a scale of one to ten, with one being very little and ten being very
much, how much peace do you have *internally*?

When have you felt the greatest peace in your life?

What are you currently doing that gives your life a real sense of peace?
What is the most important thing you could do to increase
your satisfaction and peace with yourself?

My life is my message.

— Mahatma Gandhi

What is *your* life's message?

Is your life currently sending the message you want to send?

Who are three people — famous or not — whose lives
sent a message worth learning?

When you die, what do you think your life will be remembered
for more than anything else?

If you could ensure that people would remember three things
about you and your life after you're gone,
what would you want those three things to be?

I merely took the energy it takes to pout and wrote some blues.

— Duke Ellington

How easy is it for you to turn bad situations into good ones?
Are you able to take negative energy and convert it to positive energy?

Can you think of times in your life when you've wasted a lot of energy
in the wrong areas or on the wrong things?

In the course of your life right now, where is most of your energy
being spent? Is this good or bad? Is it productive or counterproductive?

If, whenever you became angry, you could instantly channel
your emotions into something positive, what would you do?

Nothing splendid has ever been achieved
except by those who dared believe
that something inside them
was superior to circumstance.

— Bruce Barton

Do you believe, as Barton does, that great things
can only be achieved by one's ability to dominate circumstances?

Can you think of any times when you overcame
difficult circumstances to achieve something?

What circumstances do you personally find the most challenging?
Are there certain adverse situations that actually *propel* you to success?

Standing in the middle
of the road is very dangerous;
you get knocked down by traffic
from both sides.

— Margaret Thatcher

On what issues do you tend to be middle-of-the-road?
On what issues are you firmly entrenched on one side?

Do you respect people who take a firm stand for their beliefs — even
when their opinion differs radically from yours?

Do you prefer conversing with people who can swing either way on an
issue or with people who have a strong opinion and stand by it?

Across the board, do you think people should take more definitive stands on
issues, or do they need to be more willing to accept all sides and all views?

Admit your errors
before someone else exaggerates them.

— Andrew V. Mason, MD

How many times has an error you've committed been magnified
because you didn't admit to it early on?

Why are errors often exaggerated but successes downplayed?

Are you quick to find fault with other people and to point it out to them
or others? Do you tend to exaggerate their faults?

Besides the fact that someone else might exaggerate it, what are some
other reasons why it's better to confess to a mistake as soon as it happens?
Why is this sometimes so hard to do?

Has there ever been a time in your life when immediately admitting
to an error really paid off?

*I could never convince the financiers
that Disneyland was feasible
because dreams offer too little collateral.*

—Walt Disney

What are your life's dreams? Are you dreaming big or small?

Have you ever had what you thought was a great idea shot down
because others didn't think it was practical enough or didn't have
enough faith in your vision? Have you ever pushed forward
with a dream despite resistance from others?

Who are some people you know about who overcame much resistance
to make their dream come true?

How do you know when a dream is truly unrealistic and unachievable or
when it has the potential to become something real and great?

*The greatest secret of success in life
is for a person to be ready
when their opportunity finally comes.*

— Benjamin Disraeli

Do you feel like a great opportunity has ever passed you by,
or more to the point, that *you* ever let one slip by?

Do you believe that opportunities periodically come along in life or do
you think that most of us get just one big chance in life?

How do you know when the time is right for something?
Is there a certain "litmus test" you use?

How do you think one can prepare for opportunity to strike?

Do you believe that opportunities come to a person,
or must an individual go out and find them?

You must begin wherever you are.

— Jack Boland

Why do you think this statement could be hard
for many people to accept?

Do you know people who are never quite ready to do something or move
forward simply because they *think* they are not ready yet?

Do you tend to put off your goals or your dreams, thinking that there will
be a better time or a better opportunity tomorrow?

Have you ever started something even though you felt you
weren't really ready for it? What was the outcome?

If you're honest with yourself, what is something that you must begin
in life — right now, as you are — without further delay?

Choose a job you love and you will never have to work a day in your life.

— Confucius

How content are you with your current job? What, if anything, is holding you back from achieving more of what you want out of your career?

What are the three most frustrating aspects of your current job?
What are the three most enjoyable?
Does the good outweigh the bad, or vice-versa?

How much better would your life be overall if you
were truly doing what you love? Are you already?

Would you be willing to take a major pay cut in order to work
at a job that you absolutely love, or would you rather make
good money at a job where you're not happy?

Who are some people you know who absolutely love their jobs?
In each case, why do you think they do?

If you could have any job you wanted — any one at all —
which would you choose? What would be
some potential drawbacks of this perceived "dream" job?

The real moment of success
is not the moment apparent to the crowd.

— George Bernard Shaw

Why do you think Shaw would argue that our own true moment
of success is different from what others think it is?

Think of three famous people. What do you consider to be their defining
moment of success? Do you think that each of these individuals
would see this moment the same as you do?
What might *they* consider their real moment of success?

To this point in your life, what has been your defining moment
of success, in your opinion? What do you think other people might
consider — or expect — your defining moment of success to be?

What, if anything, must you still achieve for you
to deem your life wholly successful?

The whole is the sum of the parts,
so be a good part.

— Nate McConnell

Do you see yourself as a "good part" of the world?
What have you come to see as your place, or purpose, in the world?

Do you see yourself as a "good part" of your workplace?
Are you a "good part" of your family?
How would the whole be better if you were a better part?

Specifically, how have you tried, or how are you trying,
to make the world a better place?
Do you feel your small part in the world can make a difference?
Do you feel that other people have truly benefited from your existence?
Why or why not?

Always hold yourself to a higher standard than anyone else expects of you.

— Henry Ward Beecher

On a scale of one to ten, how high are your standards for yourself?
On the same scale, how high are the standards you set for other people?

Do you think others view you as a person with high standards,
average standards, or low standards?
Are they right or wrong in their assumptions?

Do you think others would do well to have your same set of standards?
Why or why not?

In what particular area of your life do you hold yourself
to the highest possible standard?

Think carefully: Did you set your standards, or did the people around
you create the set of standards you use?

Somewhere on this great world
the sun is always shining,
and it will sometimes shine on you.

— Myrtle Reed

When was the last time you really felt the "sun" shine on you?
Do you believe that everyone eventually experiences good fortune,
or are there people who will simply never know that joy?

Does it help you when you're feeling low to realize that good days will
eventually return? Does the prospect of brighter tomorrows get you through
the tough times, or do you tend to dwell on the hard rain of the moment?

If you look at your life as a whole, do you remember
more sunny moments or more dreary ones?

Are you able to celebrate someone else's good fortune or joy
even when your own life is at low ebb?

The world always steps aside
for people who know where they're going.

— Miriam Viola Larsen

Do you believe that confidence
clears the widest path through resistance?

On a scale of one to ten, how much confidence do you have in yourself?
Do you find that your confidence or lack thereof
directly affects your success?
What are you most confident about in your life right now?

What kinds of people do you find yourself stepping aside for?

*Character is doing what's right
when nobody's looking.*

— J.C. Watts

Are you more likely to do the right thing
when others are around to recognize your good deed?

Do you ever do good things only because you know that there will be
some kind of compensation given back to you (e.g., making a big
donation because it provides a helpful tax deduction or helping someone
only because you know they will pay you for your "charitable" act)?

Can you think of a specific act of goodwill that you did when nobody
was around to see it? Was it enough reward simply to know in your heart
that you had done what was right?

*We must adjust to changing times
but still hold to unchanging principles.*

— Jimmy Carter

In the last twenty years or so, what have been the three biggest changes in the world, in your opinion? Have you been willing — or able — to adjust to these changes?

What principles are a few you think we, as a people, have forsaken in recent history?

Is it really possible to adjust to changing times while still holding on to age-old principles?

Have you compromised any of your principles to fit into our rapidly changing world? Is it more important for you to fit in or to hold firmly to your own beliefs regardless of how the majority feels?

What principles will you adhere to no matter how much the world continues to change?

Success is often just an idea away.

— Frank Tyger

Do you believe this statement oversimplifies the path to success?
Why or why not?

One bestselling business book suggests that people
who want to make it to the top should spend one full hour each day
"dreaming, scheming, and thinking" and then writing down
in an "idea notebook" what they come up with.
Would you ever consider setting aside time each day
for the sole purpose of thinking?

Have you ever had an idea where you knew right away
you were on to something great?

You can't build a reputation
on what you're going to do.

— Henry Ford

What, for you, is the most difficult part of getting started on something?
Is it lack of energy? . . . lack of time?
. . . lack of confidence? . . . or something else?

What is something you've been saying for the longest time
you are *going* to do? Why haven't you done it yet?

What is something you definitely want to accomplish
within the next few years?
What specific measures must you take to actually realize this goal?

A keen sense of humor helps us to tolerate the unpleasant, overcome the unexpected, and outlast the unbearable.

— Reverend Billy Graham

Find something to laugh about.

— Maya Angelou

When was the last time you had a *really* good laugh?

Do you make it a point to laugh often? Do you put yourself in situations where laughter is both encouraged and abundant?

What are some things that make you laugh?
Do you pursue these things in your life?

Do you prefer to surround yourself with serious people or funny people?

What are some things in your life you need to take less seriously?

Do you think that improving your sense of humor
would help you get through stressful situations more easily?

Do you find that people with a good sense of humor
seem to do better in life?
Why or why not?

Pleasure is very seldom found
where it is sought.
Our brightest blazes are commonly kindled
by unexpected sparks.

— Samuel Johnson

Can you think of instances in your own life where you found joy
in something completely unexpected?

Why is it that some of our best experiences or accomplishments
in life have their beginnings in unlikely places or moments?

What was the smallest spark in your own life
that kindled a great fire within you?

*Understand the difference
between success and fame.
Success is Mother Teresa.
Fame is Madonna.*

— Erma Bombeck

Given Bombeck's definition, are you shooting for success in your life,
or are you really striving for fame?

The quotations in this book contain many different definitions
of success. If you had to write your *own* definition of success,
what would it be?

The heart has its reasons,
which reason does not know.

— Blaise Pascal

Have you ever done something your heart told you to do
even though your head warned you not to do it?

Have you ever followed your heart even though
everyone around you cautioned against it?

Do you tend to take action based more on your *heart* or your *mind?*

How big a role do feelings and emotions play in your
day-to-day decision-making process?

What's the best real-life example you know of someone
who followed his or her heart even though there were easier or less
painful paths they could have chosen?

Can you think of any particular belief you have
for which the only reason you can give is,
"I just believe in my heart that it's so"?

I only hope that we never lose sight of one thing — that it all began with a mouse.

—Walt Disney

With this statement, Walt Disney was tracing back to a mouse named
Mickey an unprecedented career in entertainment.
What particular moment or event was *your*
very first step toward success?

Why is it so important to never lose sight of our beginnings, whether it
relates to our career, our life, our nation, or anything else?

Do you feel you've come a long way from where you started?
If, back at the beginning, someone had told you that you
would make it this far, would you have believed them?

Whom do you have to thank for giving you your first big break,
whether in your career or your life in general?

If you could go back to the beginning of anything in your life,
but knew everything then that you've learned over the years,
what one thing above all others would you definitely do differently?

In three words I can sum up everything
I've learned about life: It goes on!

— Robert Frost

Yes, it does . . . life continues whether you decide to make the most of it or not. So give *this* some thought: You can dwell on the past or you can take delight in the future. You can march forward with confidence or you can stand still. You can accomplish great things or you can think small thoughts. You can make the world a better place or you can make the world a bitter place.

Here's hoping that the quotes and questions you have read in this book will inspire you to take the necessary steps toward realizing your potential, fulfilling your dreams, and at times shifting your focus away from yourself and onto others. Indeed, life *does* goes on — so get out there and make every moment you have count!

My Own Favorite Quotations

Please use the following pages to write down your own favorite
quotations, along with any questions you create that relate to them.
Whenever you hear a great new quote, remember to write it down here!

_____

_____

_____

_____

_____

_____

_____

My Own Favorite Quotations

My Own Favorite Quotations

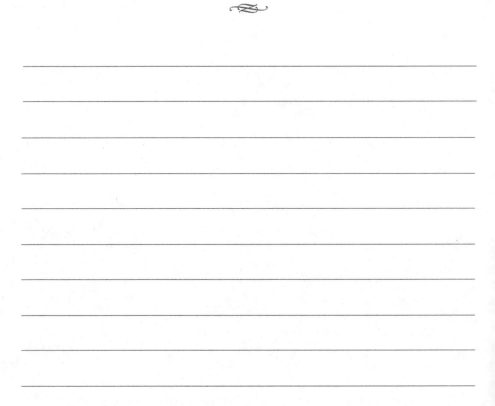

_____

_____

_____

_____

_____

_____

_____

_____

_____

My Own Favorite Quotations

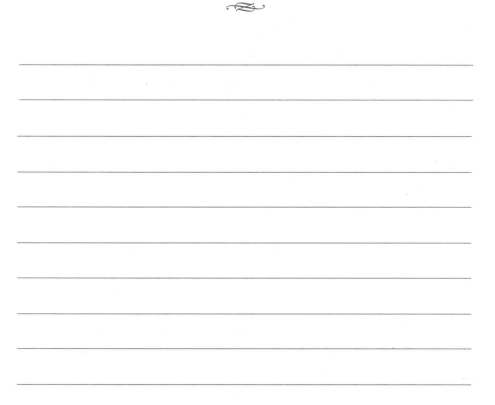

My Own Favorite Quotations

My Own Favorite Quotations

Index

About the Authors

The Question Guys™, Bret Nicholaus and Paul Lowrie, are full-time writers. They have written twelve books, including the best-selling question books *The Conversation Piece* and *The Christmas Conversation Piece*. They have also created a board game, a page-a-day calendar, and a syndicated radio show — all based on the many questions they have written. Including *Give It Some Thought,* they have penned more than 3,000 questions now in print.

Nicholaus and his family live in the Chicago area. Lowrie resides in South Dakota. Both authors are 1991 graduates of Bethel College in St. Paul, Minnesota.

To contact the authors for speaking engagements or publishing seminars, write them at the following address:

Bret and Paul, The Question Guys™
P.O. Box 340
Yankton, South Dakota 57078